AF440157

# FOR MY DAUGHTER

# For my daughter—for Xara

*Seek not wisdom beneath the branches of the mighty oak.*
*Its shadows cast confusion.*
*Stand instead beside the saplings.*
*There is more light. You will gain clarity.*

- Sister Monica Joan, *Call the Midwife*

# CONTENTS


| | |
|---|---|
| *Memories* | *1* |
| *Growth* | *29* |
| *Inspiration* | *51* |
| *Advice* | *65* |

# MEMORIES

## For My Daughter

Chop off my head and put it on your shield.
I will protect you until the day I die
And all the days after that.
You think I would let anything harm the
perfection that sprang from my body?
That force that is me and infinitely you at the
same time?
There is nothing in the world that could destroy
us,
Not when a mere glance can turn men to stone.

# First Blood

I remember the first blood of her,
The implant blood they call it.
It was possible I was pregnant,
We had laughed about it in Malta a few days
and half a world away ago,
Sitting on our private balcony in a walled city,
Drinking a bottle of wine as a cart pulled by a
horse strolled by.

We'll call her Xara, we said, for the hotel built
into the battlements where she was conceived.
The strength of old stone and softness of
embossed butter at breakfast were a foretelling
Of the child that was now in my womb,
Nestling into place with a pinprick of bright,
vibrant red.

## Of Course

Her feet were purple when she was born,
The cord pinned between her shoulder and me.
Half a dozen extra doctors and nurses had
converged in the room moments before,
All of me open to all of them
As my doctor, the one I started with so many
weeks ago,
Back when she told me they don't use the tongs
anymore,
Suction cupped her tiny head and yanked,
I breathed,
And the baby entered this world with a mighty
howl.

In seconds all the contingency actors vanished.

The center of the room, the universe,
Was a tiny creature, fists tight, mouth wide,
screaming.
Of course she was born the only way she lives—
stubborn and fearless.

## Baby Book

I didn't make my daughter a baby book,
I wrote her weird poems instead.
I can hear her explaining this to her friends,
"There's no scrapbook full of memories
But there is a special poem about me being
Athena, and one about my birth, and when I
was conceived.
My parents named me after a fancy hotel."

Dear God, what have I done?
I'm *that* mom,
The unhinged mom that really should know
better.

We don't have annual professional photos in
matching outfits,
Just the ones we take, that stop time at the
imperfect moment
The ones that capture life.
You can't get the perfect shot when you're busy
living.

Well, you can, but you have to be ready for it.
You must listen for inspiration to strike.
And when it does you take the picture, write
the poem, make the art, make the child.
And that's what we're here to leave behind, our
creation, in its imperfect divinity.

## Morning Magic

A princess sits at the edge of my bed
Telling fantastical stories,
My sleepy head tripping over the details
But in line with the nuance.
She prattles like a caffeinated sage,
Wisdom seeping out of jumbled phrases,
Bits of stories, weaving together
Her dreams, desires, realities.
It's all the same,
She speaks her life.

## Four

A sure, young voice speaks clearly
Fully of instruction
Certain and grounded
Knowing what she wants and the path to it
If this is my legacy,
I am content.

## Swim Shorts (Five)

She's wearing swim shorts
That don't fit her
And never will
Because her buns are too small
She calls it her booty
And shakes it
Which is hilarious
Because she's five
But what can you expect
Growing up in WeHo.

Will she be the first to feel true liberation?

I have felt bits of it, through her
Because it's easy not to give a damn
When you're a mom.
You have to choose,
But once you do
It takes work for them to hurt you
Because it's endlessly easy to protect her
At all costs.

Now I realize why women are so terrifying
and I love it!

So she's wearing the swim shorts
With the gaps
And heaving her dive sticks
One by one
Into the pool
And she wants them scattered
Because it's harder that way and
"Harder is more fun"
And I realize this is the point of it all,
Of this life, and all our other lives before–
She wore swim shorts.

## Good Things

She remembers that you get to pick where you
want to sit at IHOP
And she knows exactly where she wants to sit.
She notices we are wearing the same outfit
Bike shorts and shirts with sleeves that are too
big.

Two women pick their favorite booth.
She clocks their enthusiasm
Content to share the experience
Knowing the good things in life
Come easy.

## Blue Boots

It's easy to feel God when there's a hurricane
and earthquake on the same day
Reminding us she's there
In this earth, this sky,
Splashing in the puddles with the girl,
The blue boots smacking the water with
purpose
Emphatic in the chaos they conjure
As her dad cooks fish over a flame outside
In a rainstorm
Because we are ravenous
And miracles happen every day in this world.

## Mesas

We are so beautiful, inside and out
And I love that about us and all the fun we have.
Today we're flying.
We're good at that, pros, really.
We've got our snack mixes and apple juice and
Chardonnay the flight attendant didn't side eye me about
Because she gets it.

We look out the window at miles and miles of mesas
Flaunting their shadows even in the midday sun.
She wonders what a mesa is.
I tell her I think it's a mountain that the wind blew the top off
But as I say it aloud, that doesn't seem possible,
It sounds like a joke.

I tell her we should go see the Grand Canyon
next summer.
She wonders what a canyon is
And I say it's the opposite of a mountain, carved
by a river
And that sounds even more impossible than the
wind.

But we love the impossible, the improbable,
anything someone tells us can't be done.
Those are our favorite.

# Dancers

He said I have snake energy
Like living with an alligator,
That's fair.
I know what I'm like,
I like what I'm like.
Who says no to snake energy?

She said washing her hands would feel worse
than both of us dying.
She's got a flair for the dramatic.
Who knows where she gets that from,
I like that about her.

Mother snake and daughter tiger
Weaving in out and around each other
A delicate dance we execute with ease
Dare you cross our path to play.

## Sunset

We're flying west
On a jet outrunning the sun.
The mountains below
Mere bumps in the carpet.
I can see all seven colors of the rainbow,
Though I know the most intense are directly in
front,
Only visible to the pilots.

We fly all the way to the ocean
Where the water kisses the light.
I can smell the moisture in the air,
Even from way up here,
The desert inside the plane soaking up life.

An hour of sunset.

The distortion of time and light feels like
playing God,
And I'm not even flying the plane.

## Black Cats

We swallow the moon
Then eat the rainbow,
Tightening the pink bracelet on the small wrist
With a blue clay bead
To represent the other favorite color
And fall asleep under
A pastel woven blanket
From my childhood
That looks right at home here
With lavender stripes.

When all we want is to pray to the lavender
gods
Of ice cream, shoes, painted nails–
Everything that matters and is simple.

Like a black cat
Fearless
Like Elsa, but the opposite color.
Her baby perched in a chair
To protect her from the dogs
She provokes
For she is the queen of her domain,
Controlling it all with herself and nothing more.

Cat, dog, man. Man, dog, cat.
She always wins
And we search for her hiding place
Hoping she'll trust us
But she doesn't, not yet.

My baby cat sleeps in the bed
Under my blanket
Safe but wise
Ready for the dogs and the men
And the chaos we control.

## Pew Squeak

I look at a picture of an old church and hear the
pew squeak,
Smell the wood,
Feel the grit of the stone rub against my soles.

What a gift the internet—no to be specific:
social media, X, the dodgy information platform
run by a Fascist—
What a gift it has given me,
Streaming images of a 12th-century church in
England,
Bedecked in flowers placed by a Churches
Conservation Trust volunteer that very day
In this year of our Lord 2023;

Streaming images into my phone in LA while
the moon covers the sun,
And the girl uses special glasses to see it
obscured before she watches her best friend
slap a softball nearly into the outfield;

As the world descends into chaos
As before,
And it feels like a dream and it's all happened
somewhere, before.

## Meet Me Tonight

She sings Atlantic City to herself
"That's my favorite part," she'll say
As the accordion joins in
To The Band's version. It's real honky-tonk.
Where did she come from, this daughter of
mine?

## Date Brunch

Green grapefruit, just turning
Pulling down the branches, many
Near ripe to pick.
A head peeking out, bobbing the boughs
Stopping, scratching the skin to sniff, sticky
sharp oil.
Clumsy statues, her first introduction to formal
religion
A path, a garden, a story
Understanding it as her own
Her mystery, her purpose, her place on the tree.

## Good Magic

They came and hauled the agave away
Three wheelbarrows full of life that was.
Her giant root still anchored far below,
Little pups peeking out, awaiting their turn.
The super moon rises tonight
Alive not with her own light, but reflecting back
another's,
A powerful other.

What do we see when someone shines our light
back to us?
Do we shy away from the brilliance
Or bathe in the glow of life?
The point is sharpened in the mirror
Unless you squint and it all becomes blurry.
Is perspective really all it's all about?
That seems too easy
But then the good magic always is.

## She is Not Impressed

My daughter will not be impressed
With something so trivial as
Table side guac
Because she makes that at her own table,
Mortar and pestle in hand.
My little basic b witch
Taking all she can in this life.

She will never be wowed by
A man playing guitar, singing a love song
Because Elsa sang to find herself, to love herself
And she will never forget.
She never did.
Thank God there wasn't time.

A fast car
Will not awe her
She's already traveled at the speed of light
On her bike, her scooter
A lime green wiz
Zig zagging through people waking in the park,
Startled by the boldness of something so short,
Wondering at their inability to catch it
Bottle it
To savor later, when they're not self-conscious
When they stop listening to the world and start
impressing themselves.

## The Artist

My daughter stands smiling for a photo
By her art on the bathtub wall, cradling her
paints in her arms.
She is an artist.
I've known this since before she was born.

She looks at the world like an artist—
Critical, observant, fervent, hungry
Always ready to feast on color.

## Us

We're soul mates, connected over time and
other lives
To be here together now,
And he would pick our daughter over me every
time.
I would pick her too
That's why we're soul mates.


## Like Mother

Not to be dramatic but I have the most
dramatic daughter in the history of the
universe.

# GROWTH

## Measures

One of the things I love most about kids is their
inability to comprehend the measure of time
Seconds, weeks, hours, days—these words have
no meaning
Months become sooooo long and years are
short
Minutes are an eternity on this day,
But there is no saying what tomorrow will
bring.

I almost feel bad explaining it.
I don't want to call them back from some astral
plane
Where linear time means nothing.
Their world is infinite and their size at the same
time
How expansive could you be if you didn't count
the minutes but let them pass over you,
Under you,
All around you?

## To Begin

He wants to tell me the story of his life
And tugs at my sleeve for eye contact
To begin—steadily, patiently, intently
Unhurried to get to his point
Trusting you to follow down his path
Relishing the journey,
The process
Of being heard.

## Child Led

The resistance starts with children—
They are loud
They make their voices heard
They are good at asking for what they want and
need,
And they expect to get it
They find creative solutions to complex
problems
They understand that messing up and making
mistakes is part of the process
They are interested in the feelings and
emotions of others
They challenge authority, repeatedly
They speak truth to power
They question the status quo
Their primary motivation is to find joy and love
They are masters of being in the moment
They are born optimists
Their number one goal is to be happy—
Many people find these traits subversive, which
tells you a lot about society and why we must
let our children rule.

# Dandelions

Slow walks back to the car at the end of the
school day
In spring they are interminable
As our path is overgrown with dandelions
And she cannot resist picking each one to blow,
to kiss free.

Her thrill and delight never waning,
Only growing stronger with each new bloom
Fleeting friends
Forever linked
By the wonder of childhood.

## Mud Balls

It's Eden in the middle of LA
With huge shade trees,
And wandering vines
Where the light peeks through—
Streaming, diffuse, dappled, depending on the
wind and time of day.
Alchemy occurs here because children are
adept at magic,
And this place is ruled by kids.

They spend each day expanding, changing,
Turning sand into mud, mud into gold.
If you ask them why they do it
There will be one simple answer,
"To see, see what it's like to be me."
You will be amazed at the certainty they carry
in their dusty, sticky hands
And yearn to create something precious from
the clay.

Because it's your birthright, all of ours,
And the young ones have not yet forgot.
The enchantment of self discovery is still alive
When we are not worried what we may find,
When we are excited by the strange, wild,
wonderful,
When we welcome what is not us in others
And even more when we welcome what we
share,
Crouched in the dirt in the shade of a tree,
ceaselessly growing.

## Their Orbit

He rolled the Earth across the wood floor
Clunk, clink, clunk
It made itself known
She stopped its roll
And sat on it.

Her legs wrapped around it
He watched, feeling possessive of his toy
But unafraid of her designs.

They looked at one another,
Trying to discern the threat
But there was none
She rolled the Earth to him
And he sent it back to her.

## Preschool Weddings

My daughter will marry her preschool best
friend,
The one she plays with every day,
Argues with everyday,
Loves and hates everyday.

The preschoolers know
That if it's not a big feeling, it doesn't matter.
And wow, do they love the things that matter.

They're working on their issues,
Finding the exquisite balance of giving without
losing yourself.

There are two absolutes in their world,
"Piñatas make a wedding."
And
"It's important to work on these things if we're
gonna get married."
They seem to have it all figured out if you ask
me.

## The Work

I drive my daughter to school and think,
This is the work.
I see her greet her peers with gleeful hugs and
whispered understanding and think
This is the work.
I watch her twirl her friend's curl of hair gently
around her finger as they lose their train of
rational thought and dip into easy
understanding and think
This is the work.
Children come together to begin their day that
looks like play
But is really the work.

I pause for one last glance out the window
where the dust rises as their feet dance,
And it catches the light in shimmering stillness
above their heads and think
This is the work.
It's quiet inside but I can hear the larks,
increasing in intensity like thoroughbreds
barreling down the stretch to the finish that
means nothing to them,
But everything to the punter and think
This is the work.

## Ages

Patina that you feel with your fingers as you trace the serpentine lines of a Chippendale chair
Created from centuries of use
Like wooden blocks
At a school who has seen generations grow
Where students return as teachers
In name only, since learning never ceases.

Creation may crumble in your hands as the dried mud returns to sand
But this is the way.

There are new objects to forge
And perfect with the care of time.

Novel can smell old, as between pages.
Ink, always ageless,
Pens our heart to uncover secrets
And preserve until a reader
Picks them afresh
To touch back to life.

# Morning Meeting

A chalkboard with names
A chairperson
A sharing
A golden spoon for tasting soup and making
French dumplings
It has a fancy name
I forgot.

A big paper to record
With a red marker and a blue marker
Children's drawings in the margins
A plan for a rope swing, for a dance party, for
stories at the lunch table
A stuffed dog sniffing the fish tank
A slap bracelet watch not to be slapped or
thrown into the rafters where the spiders
reside,
Watching, listening.

A globe to be rolled like a ball
But not today.
Through the window a tree to climb
New chairpeople
Reluctant to leave their composition books and
find the owner of the next chalked name

Another sharing
A stuffed snowman
A baby wolf, adopted
Clothes pins, sneakily attached to the back of a
jacket—
The perpetrators not as stealthy as they
imagine.

A girl higher in the tree now
Securing a bear to the branch above her head so
the bear can climb too
The dog by the window, peering in at the faces
looking out, hands on the glass
Circling back to move forward.

Is the meeting done?
Nearly
All chalked names lined through
The chairperson declares it
And the day truly begins.

# First Sleepover

You must come over again because I forgot the
orange peel in the Negronis
And I want to bake a cake. Or some cookies for
next time
Even though the girls can barely eat
Or get through their list
Of things to do at a sleepover.

They could hardly speak at the start
And when they were watching the second ice
flick
My daughter finally found her voice
And demanded to know if she would do this
with anyone else—
Even Rebecca.

And the answer was inconclusive and that was
ok.
Because they are enough in this relationship to
understand they are together separate,
A personality of two
And then of each one.
Either version works whenever,
And each is eternal.

I cook better after you leave
In  the  hope  that  these  young  things  might
actually eat something worthwhile.
I need to see that someone else believes it.

So much of this parenting is blind faith,
Exactly like their bond of hearts that only grow,
They lead us down the path to know.

## A Color Wheel

My daughter wants to make red
She wants to know what color to use
I tell her there are none, just red makes red.

She knows that's not true
Grabs the orange and purple, scribbles on the
bathtub tile, cancels wavelengths
And makes red.

## Family Coven

A witch taught me how to channel magic
And I remembered the ancient knowledge in
my bones
In this life they cannot burn me.

Then my daughter collected all the Christmas
tree needles for her bath-time potions
And my husband asked for a molcajete
And she explained that a hex is a bad spell.

It's like they know,
To be ready.

## You're Ready

I stand at the edge of a precipice
Equipped with everything imaginable
I could ever need
Amassed over a lifetime
That I've been preparing for
Unknowingly, knowingly.

## To Climb

My daughter will climb to the highest part of
the play structure
That part you're not supposed to be able to
reach
But she's always reaching.

A part of me thinks I shouldn't let her
Because she might fall

But she knows,
She knows the precariousness of her situation,
Her perfectly balanced body high above the
ground
How a momentary lapse of concentration
would mean a fall
So she stays focused
And doesn't fall

And I realize that trusting her is trusting
myself, is trusting all of us
That we know and can manage for ourselves
No matter how high the bar.

## More

I want her to have all the things I had
And more.
More fun
More friends
More money
More lovers
More of all of it.

I want her to be bigger than me too.
I want her to be more beautiful
And more vibrant,
More admired
More fun to have at parties,
And I am pretty fun to have at a party.

I want her to know that she can be anything she
wants to be
Even if it's a bigger version of me,
A better version of me.

Even if it means having all the things I dreamed
and hoped for
And never got to have.

Even if it means doing none of the things I like
And living her life so radically different from mine
I don't even recognize it,
Or her.

All I want is for her to be the fullest expression of who she is
Because I know that will make her the most happy
In this life.

# INSPIRATION

## Me

He met me where he thought I was
And found I didn't budge.
He was confused, wrong footed,
So he blamed me,
And I still didn't give an inch.

## Me II

I make ultimate peace with my strangeness,
With my weirdness,
With all that is special inside me.

## Me III

I am old world and Californian—
The merging of the best viniculture has to offer.
Mostly I drink the old stuff though, it has more
understanding.
Like the smell off the Mediterranean at
midnight in Beirut,
A place I had never been,
And been a thousand times before.
Understanding.
That's all I'm looking for
In this life and all the others.

# Medusa

I learned about Medusa when I was small
And didn't realize we weren't supposed to like her
Or that she was scary.
If you don't want to be turned to stone,
Just don't look.

I was more concerned about unruly hair
And how did she sleep?
It seemed like a thrilling problem
I imagined names I'd give my hair snakes.

And what about the other Gorgons?
Her sisters are immortal,
And you're not gonna tell me all?

You've gotta dig for the good stuff,
The stuff they don't teach you.

## Athena

Athena is fierce in everything
And men pray to her when they are afraid
They do not want to displease her or incur her
wrath
They dread and worship her

They will dread me
Not because I am fearsome but because I hold
so much power within
What will I do with it?

It is possible to be terrifying and adored
We are born that way,
Tiny helpless beings who demand and receive.
The hunger within us is great, unrelenting
Where does it go?

That's the secret, it hasn't gone anywhere
We still hunger for sweet, sweet milk
That's the default we struggle to return to

Athena doesn't struggle
She laughs when we do
So we can too

## Aphrodite

The goddess of love sprang from the sea
perfectly formed
She is no mere mortal
She can summon wars to end kingdoms on a
whim.

You think she cares if you heed her song?
She wants you to listen to your own song,
The one inside you,
The one of love.

## Ophelia

Ophelia walked so that good girls could run
Away from the madness of a world that tries to
imprison them from first breath.

We know what we are from the start,
Even when we are green and meek.

We are discovering what we may be,
And it flows out of us like the ramblings of one
possessed.
How else to be heard above the din of men?

We know the secrets of the universe and need
to explain them in floral metaphor,
In poetry,
So you'll understand,
So anyone will understand, this—
We are infinitely powerful and the dominion
you claim is that which we have ceded you
And will one day demand back.

Until then we float on,
Adorned with flowers,
Intent in our purpose,
Unwavering in our growing strength.

## Toothbrushes

I put toothbrushes in a poem for Sylvia
Because I love her
And want to liberate her
Even though she already did it for herself
Before she died.
Don't let them tell you different,
She couldn't live without her satisfaction
Of writing a poem.
How magnificent.

## Bagpipes

There is a girl who plays the bagpipes
At the corner of Crescent Heights and Santa
Monica
And I've been aching for her to come back
And call out to my soul
Through continents and oceans and ages
And all the things we cannot measure but
Believe we can.

## Maman

I see the most amazing spider web
Stretching between two trees
And it is huge.

When the light hits it just so
It glimmers as a precious gem,
An intricate pattern that looks fragile,
But isn't.

And I realize
That's what I want to do in this life—
Make something as beautiful and impossible as
that.

## Mother

Mother is a verb.
She does, does, does.
Even when she's not moving, she holds,
Holds babies, feelings, everything that will fit in
her two arms.

She can carry the entire world if you ask her,
Especially if you say please
She can't help herself,
She is strength personified.

## Poetry Reading

After Chelsie Diane

This is a remembering
When we come together
And read our truth.
We have been doing this forever.

They have tried to stop us—
Burnt us alive, tied rocks to our ankles and
threw us in the river, locked us in cages.
So many cages.

But we didn't stop.
We can never stop,
We are right where we are.

## Speak

She speaks in poetry
Like she doesn't know another way.
Seriously, there is a soundtrack to her life.
It's not even main character energy,
It's 'I embody me' energy.

How brave to live for yourself
And all your deep, true, pure desires,
The ones underneath what you show
And even the ones under those.
Excavate your heart and find the way to live for
you.

Venture to the bottom of the well
Where it's cool and quiet,
Where the water springs from the earth—
There you will find all you need,
The poetry to speak.

# Yellow and Gold

I pray to Vincent's Sunflowers.
Their yellows and gold only ever felt like
heaven to me.
I stare at the gentle way they stand in their vase
Their heads craned in different directions
Observing, silent and still, the truth of the
world.

I did this as a child and didn't realize I was
praying,
But how holy it all seems
Now that I know
How God reveals herself to me.

# ADVICE

## An Invitation

After Alok Vaid-Menon


Let me be your invitation to another way to be.
Or let that hot man on the internet be your
invitation, (him *and* his abs)
Or the woman in the checkout line buying
pounds of smoked salmon and a case of
sparking rosé
Or the child climbing a tree,
I don't care who it is.

I just want you to know you can be anything
you want in this life,
And if you need to see someone else be it before
you, then find them.
Find them and tell them you love them because
you are them.
Thank them for daring to be the thing this
world hates the most—ecstatically,
authentically, infinitely them.

Then you do it.
You be you.
And be an invitation to another way to be.

## Carpe Diem

It took me a while to realize that carpe diem
means
Take the day,
Like literally take it,
That I could take it.

So I did.

And guess what?
They don't make you give it back.

# Good Girl

Kill the good girl and do it quickly
We've been waiting around too long
To let her live one moment more.

She was never really alive, not fully
She only existed as a made-up promise, but for
whom?
She was careful to never ask
Because the answer was too terrible.

All she wants is to die and be born again
But this time as a caterpillar and then a
butterfly
Because they can be good without trying
They are inherently good
Just as she was before she had to be a good girl.

## It's Physics

She looked down, clicked the button to unfasten the restraint, stood and floated upward
Weightless, unburdened, free
She was aware on the in breath
And already traveling miles and years to a deeper understanding with the out breath
Was it a dream?
I cannot say.
But I've heard tell of a woman uncoupling herself from every single idea that weighed her down
And catapulting into the stratosphere

## Taps

The sparrow keeps tapping at my window,
Asking to come in.
Why?
What could I possibly have in here that she
cannot find out there?
I am unnerved because I think I'm missing the
joke.
The punchline sails over my head

Tap, tap, tap.
Maybe it's not a knock but a beckoning
For me to go out there
And see the world of a sparrow
Before it's too late.

## Common Things

I drove past a man with a python sunbathing
around his neck.
I jumped a little,
Unsure if what I saw was real or somehow an
imagination.
It seemed everyday and completely out of the
ordinary at once.
I think that's what scared me,
The extraordinary things we confuse as
commonplace.

## Regret

I do not shy from regret that expands desire
For desire is holy.
Everything I want is sacred.
The same with your wants,
Your desires,
Your regrets.
Cultivate them, keep them, worship them.

## Zany

My favorite places are full of chaos
Where I can contribute to the zany atmosphere.
Sometimes my cheeks burn at the stupid thing I
did or said,
But then I remember I'm part of it.
I'm part of it!
That's the gift—
I'm creating this fantastic story that we will all
talk about some day
Or not,
It doesn't really matter
As long as it's fun while we're here.

## Sustenance

The frenzy around the fruit seller in the jewelry
district is life-affirming.
His stacked crates of pomegranates, avocados
and limes beckon to passerby—
A man wants a whole papaya
And strawberries
The full sacks weigh down his arms.

The allure of a fresh raspberry more palpable
than the fluorescent displays of cold gold
The value of sustenance is easy to feel, easy to
understand.
You can touch its form, put it in your sack,
choose the plumpest, ripest
And then eat
And it gives you life,
More life than gold.
Even if fruit does not endure like precious
metal,
It can sustain.

## Truth

Some people are afraid of truth
Because it will set them free
And the joy of freedom is terrifying.

What would you do with unadulterated happiness?
Let go of petty grievances you've carried forever?
Have you noticed how your problems become your friend?
You'd miss them if they were gone.

We are creatures of comfort,
Our worries wrap around us like a warm blanket.
We'd be naked without our strife, so we choose it again and again,
But we don't have to, and that's the truth.

# Leave Behind

Some of you are more worried about the trash
you'll leave behind
Than what you create.
I refuse to believe our impact is only as big as
our carbon footprint.

It doesn't even begin to touch the surface of our
purpose here.
Our imperfect purpose,
That has consequence and meaning
Far beyond our air miles or compost pile.

Don't be afraid to live because the world is
ending.
It has always been ending, and beginning.
Find the space on the X where you and spirit
intersect and you will know,
You will know,
How infinitely valuable you are.

## A Guide

The end. As it offers some sort of beginning to
cling to in the night
When we're unsure the path forward or any
direction, let's be honest,
And finding peace with that.
The uncertainty, the powerlessness when the
adornments are put away.

Dream in the night for awakening but do not
demand it for you are on the path and you have
always been.
Directions unknown,
But a guiding light pulling you, calling you
Until you listen and realize all along, it's you.

## Art Advice

After Susan diRende


Sign your name and get out of there.


You've given it all you have
And even if you can't feel it yet,
It's good,
Really good.


So take a deep breath in,
Close your eyes,
Smell the paint and
Revel in your creation.


You did this.
And that's why it matters,
Why it sings to me
And everyone else who knows how to listen.

## Listen

Listen better.
I am calling to you.
I'm pounding on the door
Every single day
To make you listen
To yourself.

Stop ignoring me.
I can show you the way to the things you want
And you drag your heels
Or pretend like you cannot hear me.

I am doing it for you
I am you
I love you
And you know that.
You'll remember it more
Once you start to listen.

## Your Space

It took me forty years to realize the places I
wanted access to,
Fields I wanted to work in,
Groups to belong to,
Were too serious for me.

They were populated by earnest, professional,
soulless people
That masqueraded as arbitrators of taste,
So I gave up those institutions

And found my own people who get it.
That's the trick.
It's not you, it's them.
Keep going till you find your space.

# Acknowledgements

This is for Xara, for sharing her light and trusting me to nurture it. She has inspired me from her first breath, always meeting the world with an open heart.

It's also a tribute to Dan, who has been there every step of the way, encouraging the wildness of the women who surround him. He sees my blind spots and finds the words when I have none. His deep understanding makes it all possible.

To Xara's treasured grandparents, whose endless love and wholehearted acceptance of our unique parenting journey have remained unwavering, both in spirit and in action.

To Xara's teachers, who embody the practice of respecting children and meeting people where they are so we can all flourish. Their profound empathy is changing the world.

And to Margherita, whose nurturing touch and zest for life left an indelible mark on our little bird's early days and continues to do so.

When I look at Xara I'm reminded of your steadfast support. Her truest self blooms because of your collective presence and love. Thank you for reveling in the growth with me.

## About the Author

Maggie Devers is a poet and mother who writes in the spaces between living. She believes beauty is all around us. We have to look to find it, and when we do, it is imperative to share it with those we love.

She aspires for her daughter to shine as a beacon of love and truth in the world, championing a child-led approach to foster her autonomy and authenticity in every endeavor.

Observing the beauty of growth and constant change compels Maggie to write and capture the moments. Like an artist with a brush, she cannot help herself.

Find her on Instagram @rembrandts.cure.